FIRST TIME
HOME
BUYER BOOK

FIRST TIME
HOME
BUYER BOOK

THE A TO Z GUIDE FOR HOME BUYERS

THOMAS FRANK

FOREWORDED BY RYAN J SPELTZ

CONTENTS

FOREWORD

By Ryan Speltz, Loan Originator, and Friend

I met Thomas in late 2018 via Facebook. We are in a coaching program together that teaches us to always strive for more. Thomas is the definition of striving for more! He is always looking for the next best move, so naturally writing a book was a logical step.

The knowledge that Thomas puts forth in this book is amazingly helpful for anyone striving to buy a home. It allows you to see behind the curtain of the loan process, and will greatly improve your ability to understand certain terms, definitions, and pieces of the lending puzzle.

Thomas' journey to the man he has become is a great story of strength and courage, and I encourage you to reach out and find out more about him. He is a fantastic human with a giant heart, always looking for ways to help his friends and family. This book is no exception, and I know he will welcome you in to his circle with open arms. You will be considered family the second you reach out and connect with him.

Why am I qualified to speak about a mortgage lender with such confidence? I, too, am a mortgage banker (licensed in MN, TX, FL and SC; NKLS #1277170). I have seen many good lenders, and many not so good lenders. Thomas falls into the category of the GREAT Mortgage Lenders. I have family and friends that live in Colorado, and they will most assuredly be getting Thomas's contact information from me when they reach out. With Thomas's industry leading knowledge and service, you will be hard pressed to find someone to guide you through your first home buying process.

Regards,
Ryan J Speltz
#KickButtMortgageguy
www.kickbuttmortgageguy.com
NMLS 1277170

ATTITUDE IS EVERYTHING

"Your attitude determines your altitude."
- Zig Ziglar

To accomplish what you are setting out to do, you must frame your attitude in a way that allows you to move forward. When you open your mind to new opportunities, you will be able to appreciate the process and the growth that you are experiencing.

Let's start looking at buying a home as a <u>GOAL</u>, not a dream.

Write down the words:

"I WILL BUY A HOME"

Erase all questions of not being able to from your mind! Like this book… I wrote it, and I haven't written more than a thank you card since college.

You, too, can do whatever you set your mind to!

Set your mind to:

"I WILL BUY A HOME!"

For more resources and guidance,
head on over to www.newcapfinance.com.

BUYING A HOME CAN BE STRESSFUL

"Buying a home is easy!
I never feel like bursting into tears"
- No one, ever.

I come across a lot of people who have become *extremely* stressed out about the process of buying a home.

Why does this happen?

Because their brain is telling them to stress about not knowing what is next!

With the tools in this book, you will be able to calm some of these stresses, because you will have a better understanding of what will be required of you.

You will know "enough to be dangerous."

Oh, and you will have me in your corner, and that will help you be much more than dangerous!

CREDIT SCORES ARE A SNAPSHOT IN TIME

"When you become an adult,
your GPA is replaced by your credit score"
- Unknown

Ok, let's get past all of the psychobabble and figure out how to buy a house!

When someone asks your credit score, how do you reply?

If the answer is "Not good" or "terrible," you fit right in with many of the people I speak with. Have no fear, it can be fixed. **ATTITUDE**, remember?!

I can't tell you specifics on how to fix YOUR credit score. If you want specifics, head to my website: www.

newcapfinance.com and we can chat about your situation.

Credit scores are made up of the following:

- 35% Payment History
- 30% Current Loan & Credit Card Debt (Ratios)
- 15% Length of Credit History
- 10% Types of Credit
- 10% New Credit

PAYMENT HISTORY

Pay your bills on time, have good credit scores. The longer you have made on-time payments, the less of an impact a late payment will make.

CURRENT LOANS & CREDIT CARDS (RATIOS)

What are your credit limits? How close to maxed out are your credit cards? These are questions you need to ask yourself regularly. Keeping your balances under 30% is a great start. (Example: Balance of $300 with a limit of $1000). If you can keep it under 10%, that's even better!

Pro Tip: No, you don't have to pay it down right after you cross above one of these thresholds. Whatever the Statement Balance is will be what gets reported to the credit bureaus. Figure out what the <u>Statement Date</u> is and pay the balance down before that date.

As far as loan balances go, keep making your payments on time.

LENGTH OF CREDIT HISTORY

Ideally, you have a credit history length that represents longer than 2 years.

"But Thomas, I've been using credit for 10 years! Why is my average so low?"

Well, your age of credit history consists of open accounts that were on your report over the last two years. So that car loan you paid off in 2014 doesn't count. And neither does the car you bought at the "buy here, pay here" place down the road. They generally don't report your payments to credit.

TYPES OF CREDIT

A good credit report shows a mix of credit cards, loans, and a mortgage.

**<u>DO NOT TAKE ON DEBT TO FIX
YOUR CREDIT SCORE.</u>**

Did I make that big and bold enough? I have heard way too many horror stories of people going and buying a car with a 20% interest rate to try and fix their credit only to end up not being able to cover the giant payment they just took on, and the cycle continues.

If you use credit cards responsibly, you can increase your score to get you into a good place to buy a home.

NEW CREDIT

This section considers all the things that have recently been applied for (inquiries) and recently opened. Generally, not having more than 5 inquiries in a 12-month period is a good strategy. A mortgage company will ask you to explain any inquiries on your report from the last 120 days.

Bottom Line: Your credit won't be fixed overnight, but if you put these tips into action right now, you can start to dig yourself out of the credit score dungeon. Attitude is *everything*!

For more resources and guidance,
head on over to www.newcapfinance.com.

DISCOUNT POINTS

"Discount Points are like your golf score,
the lower the better"
- Unknown

Discount points are defined as pre-paying interest to get a better interest rate.

Example: Your lender quotes you a 5% interest rate with no discount points on your $200,000 mortgage. The lender should also provide you with the opportunity to "buy down" your rate with discount points. In this example, your lender says by paying a 1% discount, your rate can become 4.5%.

Math: You have prepaid $2,000 worth of interest (1% of $200,000) to save $61 per month. To decide if this is a good investment, take the dollar amount of the discount provided, divided by the monthly payment savings. In our example:

$2,000 (discount) ÷ $61 (Monthly Savings)
= 32.78 Months to recoup cost

Are you going to live in your home for 3 years or longer? Then paying discount points may make sense for you.

This scenario can also play out in a way often described as a "Lender Credit."

So, you take 1% in Lender Credit towards your closing costs, and take a higher rate than the original 5% (let's call this 5.5% for the example). The lender then applies $2,000 towards your closing costs.

If you are tight on funds to close, this might be the right decision for you.

For more resources and guidance,
head on over to www.newcapfinance.com.

EARNEST MONEY DEPOSIT

*"An Earnest Money Deposit is like the
marriage proposal of the home buying process"
– Unknown*

An Earnest Money Deposit is a deposit made when your offer on a home has been accepted. Also known as a "Good Faith Deposit," this money shows the seller that you fully intend to buy their property. The seller will then remove the listing from the market while you, as a buyer, go through the mortgage process.

Earnest Money Deposits can be any amount of money depending on the geographics, type of loan, competitive offer situation, etc. You can use these as a tool to strengthen your offer by increasing this amount.

Most often these are around 1% of the sales price, and the money is credited towards your down payment and/or closing costs.

For more resources and guidance,
head on over to www.newcapfinance.com.

FACTS ARE THE NAME OF THE GAME

*"Facts do not cease to exist
because they are ignored."*
- Aldous Huxley

When buying a home, emotions can take over and make you forget or ignore the facts.

I am a very fact-based person, and this allows me to assist homebuyers in navigating the emotional land mines that can come up.

In a loan process, it's not *IF*, it's *WHEN* something will come up as a roadblock.

Having a fact-based loan originator on your side allows your mind to relax because you know the facts are taken care of!

For more resources and guidance,
head on over to www.newcapfinance.com.

GET TO WORK EARLY

"By failing to prepare, you are preparing to fail."
– Benjamin Franklin

No, I don't mean show up at 7:45 for your 8:00 shift (though you should do that anyway). By saying "Get to work early," I am telling you that beginning to work a plan earlier will create much less stress when it's time to move. Planning out your home purchase as soon as you start thinking you want to buy allows you much more time, flexibility and options. (By reading this book, I am assuming you want to buy, right?)

Getting with a Mortgage Loan Originator (that's me!) early on, can save you a lot of misinformation, headaches, confusion, and putting your efforts in the wrong direction.

If you are interested in getting a custom plan designed for your home purchase, head to www.newcapfinance.com and ask us about the '#NewCap Path to Home Ownership'

For more resources and guidance,
head on over to www.newcapfinance.com.

HOMEOWNER'S INSURANCE IS AN IMPORTANT PIECE OF THE PAYMENT PUZZLE

"Insurance is the only product both the seller and the buyer hope is never actually used."
– Unknown

Homeowner's insurance is a policy that protects you if there is ever damage to your home. Every mortgage lender will require you to carry a policy that covers the loan amount (or sometimes full rebuild cost) on your home.

When you close on your home, the premium will be divided by twelve and become part of your monthly mortgage payment (also called <u>escrowing</u>).

As a lender, this is important because quotes can vary from company to company and house to house. I always encourage to buyers get a homeowner's insurance quote before putting in an offer so they know what the payment will look like.

For more resources and guidance,
head on over to www.newcapfinance.com.

INTEREST
(THE ONLY CURSE WORD IN THE BOOK)

"Compound Interest is the most powerful force in the universe."
- Albert Einstein

Interest is the money you pay for borrowing money.

Everyone has heard or seen an advertisement saying "Low-Interest Rates"

But what does that even mean? When you borrow money, the bank charges you for it!

The longer the term you borrow the money, the more interest you will pay.

This is important to pay attention to when getting a mortgage. Interest rate is important, but pay attention to the term, fees, and whether it is fixed, or variable.

Rate isn't always the most important if you know the strategies to beat your rate.

For more resources and guidance,
head on over to www.newcapfinance.com.

JOIN THE #NEWCAP EMAIL LIST

Joining this list will help you get weekly tips and tricks that will assist you with your home buying journey!

Join *now* at www.newcapfinance.com/newsletter

For more resources and guidance,
head on over to www.newcapfinance.com.

KEEP EVERYTHING THE SAME

"The key to success is consistency."
– Zak Frazer

Changes to your financial situation during the loan process can be devastating to your qualification. Everyone knows not to buy a car while you are in the process of closing on your home (though, some still do...), but what about the furniture store you visit that offers a payment plan?

This **will** go on your credit report!

Any inquiries acquired throughout the process will require a letter of explanation before closing. If a new debt has been taken on, your file will have to go back to underwriting.

Many will try and go around using credit and will instead use a large sum of cash to purchase something. This isn't a great idea. Sometimes, your approval is dependent on having reserves in your account after closing.

Lastly, but no less importantly, if you change jobs during the process of buying, you may have just ended your shot at that dream home.

For more resources and guidance,
head on over to www.newcapfinance.com.

LOAN TO VALUE RATIO

"The ache for home lives in all of us, the safe place where we can go as we are and not be questioned."
– Maya Angelou

Loan to Value (LTV) Ratio is the other ratio that not many people talk about. This ratio affects your debt-to-income ratio, your interest rate, your cash out of pocket and your total monthly payment.

Most loans today involve loan to value ratios that approach 100%.

USDA is a 100% LTV Loan.

FHA is a 96.5% LTV Loan.

Conforming Loans can go up to 97% LTV.

VA is a 100% LTV Loan.

Loan to Value is simply your Loan amount divided by the value of the house.

There are many low-down payment loans available.
To hear more, reach out to me at www.newcapfinance.com

MORTGAGE INSURANCE PREMIUM

"Mortgage Insurance can be looked at as a tool to get you into the real estate game without saving a fortune"
— Unknown

Mortgage Insurance is a fee that banks (or government organizations) charge when you offer a down payment of less than 20%.

You will see offers for "No MI" loans. All this means is the lender is paying your MI for you.

Your Interest rate will be higher because the lender will need to pay for this cost out of the lender credit described previously.

On government-insured loans (USDA and FHA), the mortgage insurance premium is a fixed cost (you pay an up-front premium and a monthly premium). The monthly mortgage insurance premium cannot be paid upfront by the lender. VA Loans do have an up-front funding fee, but no monthly mortgage insurance.

On conforming/conventional loans, the mortgage insurance is paid to a third-party company. This can be lender paid (as described above), paid all at once by the buyer, financed into the loan (in specific circumstances) or paid monthly.

For more resources and guidance,
head on over to www.newcapfinance.com.

NO SUCH THING AS FREE MONEY

*"Opportunity is missed by most people because
it is dressed in overalls and looks like work."*
– Thomas Edison

When you start researching, planning and speaking with real estate professionals, you will come across many offers that seem too good to be true.

They generally are!

Here are a few phrases you may see:

- "No MI"
- "Down Payment Assistance"
- "No Cost Loan"
- "No Closing Costs Mortgage"
- "No Money Out of Pocket"
- "No Fees"

All of these statements imply that you will get something, for nothing. These things can cost you much more in the long run, because the payment is coming in a form that favors the lender or another interested party.

If you are looking for a lender who will tell you like it is and make sure the scenario is truly better for you, go here: www.newcapfinance.com.

OPEN AND HONEST

"Honesty is the first chapter in the book of wisdom."
– Thomas Jefferson

Being open and honest with your mortgage professional is very critical to your success in buying a home with a mortgage.

Attempting to hide or leaving out details is a no-no, as almost all things will be found by the underwriter during the process.

An experienced mortgage loan originator will be able to use the information you give him and come up with solutions within the guidelines, but only if they know about it! We can't help if we don't know!

Another important point is to say what you want, because it may be doable.

If you don't say what you want, you might not get it!

Be transparent, and expect the same in return. My job is to see the potential pitfalls, tell you that they are there, then work with you to build bridges over them!

For more resources and guidance,
head on over to www.newcapfinance.com.

PRE-APPROVAL & PRE-QUALIFICATION

*"Pre-Approval is the most important step
in your home buying journey."
- All Lenders*

You will hear these two terms used almost interchangeably amongst real estate professionals.

The true difference:

- *Pre-approval* is when your loan application, credit report, and documents have been reviewed by an underwriter. (Paystubs, W2s, Tax Returns, Bank Statements, etc)
- *Pre-Qualification* is when your loan application, credit report, and documents have been reviewed by a loan originator. (This is most common)

If you were handed a letter from a lender, make sure to ask which you have. Is it a Pre-Approval or a Pre-Qualification?

This document will be necessary for you to make an offer on a home, and to ensure you aren't spending money without knowing you can buy that home!

Also, if you were given a letter without providing documents... RUN, don't walk on over to www.newcapfinance.com and let's talk.

QUALIFYING RATIOS (DEBT-TO-INCOME)

*"When you borrow too much money,
you are robbing your future self."*
– Nathan W Morris

Many people have come to me saying their "debt-to-income ratio" (DTI) is too high to qualify."

To fully understand this statement, we must first figure out what DTI is made of.

DTI consists of <u>Debt and Income.</u>

"WOW! Thank you, Thomas, for breaking the code."

Ok, I get it… hear me out though! Is the ratio the problem or is it one of the two things that make up the ratio?

Gross Income: Are you making enough money to qualify (or afford) what you want to qualify for? No? Can you make a change to make more (i.e. ask for a raise, find a new job in the same industry with higher pay, etc.)?

If you can't make a change with your income, can you sell that motorcycle to ditch that payment? Can you refinance your car to get a lower payment?

The basic answers to fixing Debt-To-Income Ratio:

More Income, or less Monthly Debt!

For more resources and guidance,
head on over to www.newcapfinance.com.

REAL ESTATE AGENTS ARE IMPORTANT!

*"A Real Estate Agent is the most valuable person
you don't have to pay for as a buyer."
- Unknown*

Many people approach a home purchase without a Real Estate Agent, and think they will get a better deal because of it. Often, home builders will reinforce this idea.

The truth is, that when you enter a home purchase transaction without a Real Estate Agent, the seller is licking their chops!

WHO is going to *protect* YOU?

You wouldn't try and switch the engine out on your car by yourself unless you are a professional, so why would you want to take on the most expensive purchase of your life without someone in your corner who is qualified to handle it?

All top agents will have qualified professionals in their Rolodex for your needs throughout the transaction. (Lender, inspector, air conditioning, etc.)

I work with an amazing network of realtors across the country as well. Reach out at www.newcapfinance.com and I will connect you.

SETTLEMENT STATEMENT (CLOSING DISCLOSURE)

"Can't you see it all makes perfect sense,
expressed in dollars and cents, pounds shillings and pence,
can't you see it all; makes perfect sense."
- Roger Waters

At your closing, you will sign a settlement statement that is called a *Closing Disclosure*.

This is the lender's version of a settlement statement. It will break down all of the fees and costs associated with your purchase.

Here, I will break down the different pages and sections for you:

- **Page 1** shows information regarding the date of closing, borrower names, seller names, and basic loan information. It shows loan terms, projected payments for all years of your loan, and total closing costs/cash to close.

- **Page 2** is your closing cost details.
- **Section A** contains the loan origination costs. This includes discount points, application fees, underwriting fees, processing fees, and all lender fees.
- **Section B** shows services borrower did not shop for. These costs are requirements of the loan but have been chosen by the lender on your behalf. Fees that are included are; appraisal, credit report, flood determination, verifications, etc.
- **Section C** lists services borrower did shop for. These are fees that may or may not be required but are fees of third-party companies chosen by the borrower (or by the title company chosen by the borrower). These fees include pest inspection fees, survey fees, title insurance, title search, etc.
- **Section D** displays total loan costs. It is the total of Sections A, B, and C.

Bottom Half of Page 2:

- **Section E** is for taxes and other government fees. These fees are the fees that the government collects to process a transaction. These include transfer taxes, recording fees, intangible taxes, etc.

- **Section F** is prepaid's. This section is all about things that are paid at closing to keep your bills current. These are not fees, but include homeowner's insurance, mortgage insurance, property taxes (city, county, state) and prepaid interest (daily interest paid from closing until the 1st of the month).
- **Section G** lists the initial escrow payment at closing. This section involves putting enough money into the escrow account so when the next bill comes due, there is enough money in the account. This section includes homeowner's insurance (generally 3 months), property taxes (city, county, state, 2-15 months) and mortgage insurance (generally one month).
- **Section H** is the other fees section. This includes all of the fees that don't fit into the headings defined above. This can include HOA fees, home inspection fees, home warranty fees, real estate commissions (on seller side), etc.
- **Section I** is named total other costs and totals all the borrower paid costs from sections F, G, H.
- **Section J** is titled total closing costs and adds all borrower-paid closing costs (D + I).
- **Page 3:** The calculating loan costs at the top shows a before and after of what has changed from your most recent loan estimate that was

signed. This is a confirmation that the lender has not violated fee tolerances.

- **Summaries of Transactions** breaks down and clarifies that the property taxes, adjustments, other credits, etc. balance out through the transaction. This is where you will see that the seller has paid for the property taxes while they lived in the home.

- **Final Calculations** finishes out this page at the bottom.

- **Page 4** shows additional information about the loan. Assorted loan disclosures and a breakdown of your escrow account are also placed here.

- **Page 5** has a breakdown of Total Interest Paid for your loan and contact information of the parties involved in your transaction.

As you can see, there is a *ton* of information involved with the closing disclosure. Your lender should explain the fees and layout of your closing disclosure in a way you can understand!

The law states that you must see an initial form of your CD three business days before closing. This timeline is provided so that you, as the buyer, can make sure that you understand and agree to the terms of the loan.

For an example of the closing disclosure and visual walkthrough visit www.newcapfinance.com.

TITLE COMPANIES

The title company chosen to represent you is also an important cog in the wheel. This company works closely with the lender throughout the transaction. They will do a title search to make sure there are no issues with your deed and title to your home and land.

Title is *your right to own or use your property.* Title also establishes any limitations on those rights.

The title company (or the insurer they use) will also insure your title for the future in case someone from the past claims they have a lien on your property. These battles can become very expensive to fight. Title Insurance companies will pay for that battle up to the value of your policy instead of you losing your home.

I work with an awesome group of title companies throughout the country. Head on over to www.newcapfinance.com and contact us to find the best one in your area.

UNDERSTAND WHAT YOU ARE GETTING INTO

"Knowing yourself is the beginning of all wisdom."
– Aristotle

The benefits of homeownership are plentiful!

I'm going to list a few of my personal favorites:

- Every dollar of principal I pay is a dollar that I will get back when I sell.
- I can fully customize my home to my liking.
- I have a fixed monthly cost and no landlord to raise it.
- I am building future wealth by making my mortgage payment.
- I have a place for my family to create memories and grow together.

These benefits are just a start in the plentiful world of homeownership. Owning a piece of land is one of the oldest joys in the world, and the financial benefits that come with it are great as well!

What are you most looking forward to?
Write it down, snap a picture, and tag us on
Facebook @ www.facebook.com/NewCapFinance

VALUE: THE GREAT EQUALIZER

"Price is what you pay, Value is what you get."
– Warren Buffet

Choosing a mortgage professional is difficult. Not only do you have to understand the financial impact of your decisions, but you must also understand the future impact of using this professional.

Is this person going to follow up with you year after year and make sure your mortgage is still in line with your goals?

Is this person going to send you newsletters and updates when important things happen in the mortgage and/or real estate industry?

Is this person going to give you access to your home valuation monthly, so you can see the advantages of utilizing a cash-out refinance or selling your home and moving up?

Hint: The team at New Capital Finance does all of these things.

Therefore, I call value "The Great Equalizer." If you are buying purely on price, you don't get these things. If you simply compare the numbers, and not the professionals, you are missing a large piece of the puzzle!

To view more value we provide,
head on over to www.newcapfinance.com.

WARRANTIES FOR YOUR HOME CAN SAVE YOU TONS OF MONEY

Home warranties protect you against the failure of some of your major systems and appliances.

None of us know when these systems or appliances will fail, and homeowner's insurance doesn't cover these failures.

However, not *every* homeowner needs to have a home warranty plan!

The benefit of these warranties can far outweigh the costs, which are $300-$600+ per year, and you can even get these warranty plans negotiated into the purchase agreement.

What a deal!

Don't just jump on any home warranty plan, though. Make sure you work with a trusted company with a lot of history. We can help you with this at www.newcapfinance.com.

XTRA CREDIT

Other Common Mortgage Definitions

Adjustable-Rate Mortgage - An adjustable-rate mortgage, known as an ARM, is a mortgage that has a fixed rate of interest for only a set period of time, typically one, three or five years. During the initial period, the interest rate is lower, and after that period it will adjust based on an index. The rate thereafter will adjust at set intervals.

Annual Percentage Rate - is the rate of interest that will be paid back to the mortgage lender. The rate can either be <u>a fixed rate or adjustable rate</u>.

Amortization - the amortization of the loan is a schedule on how the loan is intended to be repaid. For example, a typical amortization schedule for a 15-year loan will include the amount borrowed, the interest rate paid and term. The result will be a month breakdown of how much interest you pay and how much is paid on the amount borrowed.

Appraisal - is conducted by a professional appraiser who will look at a property and give an estimated value based on physical inspection and comparable houses that have been sold in recent times.

Closing Costs- These are the costs that the buyer must pay during the mortgage process. There are many closing costs involved ranging from attorney fees, recording fees and other costs associated with the mortgage closing.

Construction Mortgage - when a person is having a home-built, they will typically have a construction mortgage. With a construction mortgage, the lender will advance money based on the construction schedule of the builder. When the home is finished, the mortgage will convert into a permanent mortgage.

Equity - the difference between the value of the home and the mortgage loan is called equity. Over time, as the value of the home increases and the amount of the loan decreases, the equity of the home generally increases.

Escrow - at the closing of the mortgage, the borrowers are generally required to set aside a percentage of the yearly taxes to be held by the lender. Every month, the lender will also collect additional money to be used to pay the taxes on the home. This escrow account is maintained by the lender who is responsible for sending the tax bills regularly.

Fixed-Rate Mortgage - is a mortgage where the interest rate and the term of the loan are negotiated and set for the life of the loan. The terms of fixed-rate mortgages can range from 10 years to up to 30 years.

Loan Estimate - an estimate by the lender of the closing costs that are from the mortgage. It is not an exact amount; however, it is a way for lenders to inform buyers of what is needed from them at the time of closing of the loan.

Mortgage - is the loan and supporting documentation for the purchase of a home. Mortgage lenders generally follow strict underwriting guidelines to limit the possibility of borrowers defaulting on their payments.

Origination Fee - when applying for a mortgage loan, borrowers are often required to pay an origination fee to the lender. This fee may include an application fee, appraisal fee, fees for all the follow-up work and other costs associated with the loan.

Principal - is the term used to describe the amount of money that is borrowed for the mortgage. The principal amount that is owed will go down when borrowers make regular monthly or bi-weekly payments.

Settlement Costs - prior to closing, the attorneys involved in the mortgage closing will meet to determine the final costs that are associated with the loan. These settlement costs are given to all parties so that they will be prepared to pay the closing costs that have been agreed upon.

Title Insurance - the lender is using the home as collateral for the mortgage transaction. Because of this, they need to be certain that the title of the property is clear of any liens which could jeopardize the mortgage. So, lenders will require borrowers to get title insurance on the property, which will ensure that the home is free and clear.

Truth in Lending - is a federal mandate that all lenders must follow. There are several important parts to the Truth in Lending regulations, including proper disclosure of rates, how to advertise mortgage loans and many other aspects of the lending process. These regulations were put in place to protect consumers from potential fraud.

For more help with mortgage terms,
you can reach me at www.newcapfinance.com.

YOU ARE THE MOST IMPORTANT PIECE OF THE WHOLE PUZZLE

"Don't be pushed around by the fears in your mind.
Be led by the dreams in your heart."
– Roy T. Bennett

Without your effort, none of what you have read matters. Remember that you accomplish what you focus on, so focus on buying a home and it will happen!

You have the *power* to buy a home.

You have the *ability* to buy a home.

Allow yourself to do it!

Always remember that by having this book, you have a support team built-in.

The team at New Capital Finance is here to guide you to the end. From start to finish, we will be here to answer your questions, direct you to a smart financial decision, and point you in the right direction when it comes to other industry professionals.

USE US!!
www.newcapfinance.com

Z

ZOOM INTO YOUR PROCESS AND LET'S MAKE IT A SUCCESSFUL ONE!

"Imperfect action is better than perfect inaction"
– Harry Truman

Taking some sort of action to get closer to your goal is the most important step.

If you aren't willing to reach out and ask for help, it will be tough for you to get there! You may be only a couple of items being paid off, a couple more dollars, a couple more months of credit history away from being able to purchase your home.

I encourage you to zoom into the process head-on. If you commit, you will get there! I see it every day from people who didn't believe they could buy, then we build a plan and they are there in 3 months!

Crazy, right?

Get out there and do it!

www.newcapfinance.com will be there for you. Jump on over and see what quality information you can find. There is a ton of stuff there just waiting for you to consume it! Don't forget to sign up for the newsletter!

- Thomas Frank
NMLS #14017

CPSIA information can be obtained
at www.ICGtesting.com
Printed in the USA
BVHW041222151120
593363BV00016B/1016

9 781714 413737